japaneseness

japaneseness

a guide to values and virtues

yoji yamakuse

Stone Bridge Press • Berkeley, California

Published by
Stone Bridge Press
P. O. Box 8208, Berkeley, CA 94707
tel 510-524-8732 • sbp@stonebridge.com • www.stonebridge.com

This book is an adaptation of 日本人のこころ *[Nihonjin no kokoro]: Heart and Soul of the Japanese*, © 2014 Yoji Yamakuse and IBC Publishing, Inc. (Tokyo, Japan). The revised English text is based on a translation by Michael A. Cooney.

English adaptation © 2016 Stone Bridge Press.

Cover and book design by Peter Goodman.

Printed in the United States of America.

p-ISBN: 978-1-61172-026-6
e-ISBN: 978-1-61172-917-7

contents

MOKUJI

Develop Virtue 113

Appreciate Beauty 123

publisher's preface

はじめに

HAJIME NI

To the Western world and to its Asian neighbors, Japan has presented many different faces over the centuries: friend, enemy, artist, craftsman, purveyor of pop culture, high-tech wizard. Like every nation and culture, Japan has never been just one entity, although its distinctive social cohesion and normative behaviors at times make outsiders feel they are dealing with an obdurate and single-minded monolith.

The world's fascination with Japan coupled with Japan's ability to absorb and recast its old traditions into one modern form after another insures that Japan remains very much a part of our international environment. We like what is new about Japan, but we also like how many things from Japan seem to carry something older, and weightier, something distinctly "Japanese." In our dealings with Japanese people, from all walks of life, we sense that they embody something of their nation that goes far beyond citizenship. There is a sense of strong bonds between friends and workers, duty to one's family and long-dead ancestors. Whether we are talking about food, architecture, religion, sex, art, clothing, or gizmos, we are aware of a certain, in a word, "Japaneseness"— the quality of being Japanese—that signals not only the tradition and culture from which those things emanated but presages our experience of them tactilely and emotionally.

We must emphasize that this book is not meant to be a reductionist interpretation to prove Japanese "uniqueness." *All* countries and cultures have something unique in their value systems. Japan is no more distinct, no better, no more real than any place else on earth. Japan has also had a long and close relationship with other Asian cultures and value systems, particularly China's, and quite a few of those "foreign" values have found nourishment in Japanese soil and become deeply embedded in the Japanese psyche.

But Japan, an island nation for all its existence that then *deliberately* isolated itself from the rest of the planet for some two hundred and fifty years from the seventeenth to nineteenth centuries, has had a chance to incubate its value system and develop enduring and idiosyncratic forms. When modernism finally came, Japaneseness was not swept away but became absorbed into modern life, making Japan's modern life at once strange and familiar to us.

There have as a result been innumerable attempts to explain Japan and especially to enlighten the West about traditional Japanese thought and the country's value system— that is, "the heart of Japan" or its "Japaneseness."

These efforts are exemplified by Inazo Nitobe's *Bushido: The Soul of Japan* (1899) and Tenshin Okakura's *Book of Tea* (1906) and by more modern works like *The Chrysanthemum and the Sword* (1946) by Ruth Benedict, written during World War II to explain the Japanese enemy to the American people, and Takeo Doi's *The Anatomy of Dependence* (1971), which analyzed interpersonal and group relationships in Japan.

One thing shared by all these works is an emphasis on "obligation" and "duty" as central principles in the Japanese value system. But where did these values come from, and what place do they really have in modern Japanese life?

In this book author Yoji Yamakuse takes up seventy-six identifiable aspects of modern Japaneseness. Originally he wrote this book for Japanese people seeking to explain themselves and their culture to their non-Japanese friends. We are here re-casting that discussion slightly for an audience outside Japan. In doing so, we are not merely hoping, as the author does, that this text will lead to better international understanding. We also hope that this book will illuminate for many admirers of Japanese things some of the deeper aspects of the culture from which those things arose. And we are especially hopeful that these traditional Japanese values and virtues, so intimately tied to Japanese behavior and cultural endeavors, will shed light on what it means to be a human being and will offer readers everywhere fresh but time-tested tools for solving problems, getting along with each other, appreciating nature, and making new toys and technologies.

Stone Bridge Press
Berkeley, California

on reading
the japanese heart

NIHON NO KOKORO

Harmony (*wa*) is the principal value in the Japanese system. By positioning it in the center, showing its relative relation to other values, we get the illustration here.

In every culture, when its constituent values coexist and function together without friction, the people who belong to that culture feel a sense of tranquility.

For the Japanese, harmony represents tranquility, and in order to achieve it a typical Japanese person, consciously or not, will adhere to the various values, virtues, norms, and moral precepts described in this book.

In Japan, a person who embodies the totality of values inherent in the core value of harmony is a person of virtue, and this great virtue is consistent with the Japanese ideals of beauty.

Refer to this illustration while reading this book so that you can understand how each value is linked to the others.

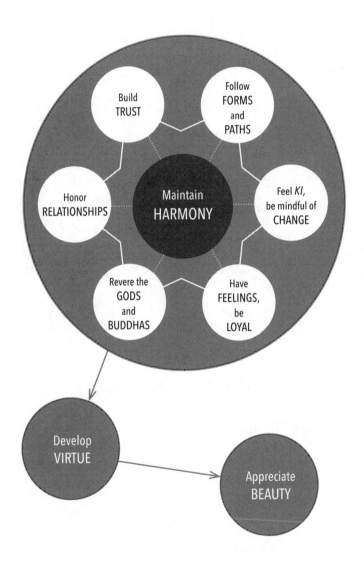

Maintain
Harmony

harmony

WA

Harmony is the key to the Japanese value system. Avoiding conflict, being mindful of the needs of others, creating a basis for mutual cooperation—these are the foundation of the Japanese approach.

The Chinese character *wa* means "harmony" and is also used to mean "Japan." For example, Japanese cuisine is known as *wa-shoku* and Japanese clothing is known as *wa-fuku*.

"Harmony" is a basic value defined as the ability of people to cooperate and work together well.

Japan is a country whose traditions developed out of an agricultural society where people were forced to work closely together on a limited amount of land. In order to maintain this type of society, the needs of the village were more important than the needs of the individual, as all labored together to plant the rice and harvest the crop.

Some anthropologists suggest that therefore, in contrast to hunter- or immigrant-based societies, where a high value is placed on the power or actions of the individual, a society developed in Japan where value is placed on understanding those with whom one must interact and on taking action in groups. That is the definition of *wa*.

Wa is at the heart of what has been necessary to nurture

everything in the Japanese value system. (See the diagram on page 13).

hospitality

Harmony is achieved by the attitude with which you approach other people. First put yourself in their place and with all your heart understand how they feel and what they need.

おもてなし
OMOTENASHI

Omotenashi means to treat or entertain someone sincerely and warmheartedly, whether that person is a visiting guest, a business contact, or a friend or acquaintance. Hospitality exists in every country: whenever an important person is received, every preparation is made to assure that the guest enjoys him- or herself.

So what distinguishes the Japanese hospitality from that found in other countries?

At the core of *omotenashi* is attentiveness to the needs of others (*ki o tsukau*). To be attentive means to read the atmosphere, sense the mood, and feel the invisible energy suffusing an occasion. To treat someone well, or to entertain a person as a guest, therefore means to create a comfortable ambiance, the conditions that enable a guest to feel at ease and relaxed.

Ultimately, it means that you do not entertain your guest to achieve some kind of self-satisfaction, but that you are quick to perceive your guest's needs and desires and the overall mood, and to entertain him or her accordingly.

During the affluent bubble period of the 1980s, when Japan was looming large on the world stage as an economic powerhouse, Japanese often went too far in keeping their foreign guests up late at night drinking pricey liquor and eating expensive food; by trying to impress their guests they ended up distancing themselves from the true meaning of *omotenashi*. Worse, hosts sometimes went too far in pushing the uniqueness of Japanese culture on their visitors from overseas.

With the passage of time and changed (more humbling) circumstances, the true meaning of *omotenashi* is now being re-examined in Japan.

thoughtfulness

Hospitality and thoughtfulness are one and the same. By anticipating someone else's needs before your own and making them your priority, you create a bond of warmth and respect.

Kikubari means to be mindful of all the delicate aspects of an occasion and to control and adjust your behavior accordingly. *Kikubari* is shown through action. It begins with attentiveness (*ki o tsukau*) and ends in showing consideration. In other words, *kikubari* is the behavior resulting from paying attention to the feelings of others. It is an inconspicuous sign of affection, an unobtrusive indication of fellow feeling.

Let's say you wish to be considerate of another's circumstances, but you do so in a rather obvious way: paying for their meal, for example. The result may be that the other person feels a sense of obligation and perhaps some emotional discomfort. If you are a truly considerate person, you might instead excuse yourself to go to the restroom and on the way catch the waiter to tell him you will settle the check separately and not to bring it to the table. Your goal is to make sure that there is a continuous feeling of well-being on the part of your guest and that nothing will disrupt the mood of the occasion. It is this type of unobtrusive consideration that lies at the heart of hospitality (*omotenashi*).

The Japanese people have long lived on the islands of Japan without much intercourse with other peoples. As a result, they have developed means of understanding one another without explicitly verbalizing their thoughts. This has given rise to the attentiveness seen in *ki o tsukau*, the unique product of a tightly knit community. The conscious consideration for others shown in *kikubari* is part of the value system of a tight community, passed down from one generation to the next.

modesty

KENJŌ

You display the spirit of harmony by deferring to others, by avoiding ostentation, and by realizing that you don't know everything and that there is much to learn from others.

If *wa* ("harmony") is to exist at the core of a relationship, things will not go smoothly if both parties egotistically emphasize their own capabilities. A Japanese person will strategically downplay his own capabilities while paying respect to the other person's. This attitude of putting oneself below another and not presuming to show your strengths is called *kenjō*.

You thus cannot take someone's words at face value when he tells you: "I don't know anything." In Japan, the greater a person's capabilities, the more modestly he will state them; such modest persons are respected all the more.

The concept of modesty is often used when introducing a member of your family or company. This is evident in the phrase "good-for-nothing son" when introducing your child, for example. Needless to say, many non-Japanese brought up in more straight-talking cultures find such expressions a bit too self-deprecating and are not impressed.

"The heavier the stalk of rice, the more its head is lowered" is an expression well liked by the Japanese. "A wise hawk hides its talons" is another popular phrase.

space, interval

間

MA

Don't be hasty but leave room for you
and others to find a meeting of the minds.
Sometimes it's best to listen and not express a point of view.
Leaving space for each to accommodate the other is key to
the Japanese heart.

Ma means an empty space or an interval between two objects or events.

Traditionally, the Japanese had a strong sense of the distance between people in terms of time and physical space. For example, during feudal times (the 14th–17th centuries) it was taboo for a low-ranking person to approach a person of high rank. Etiquette required that one speak to such persons from a considerable distance and from a physically lower position. It was common, in fact, to not approach such persons directly at all but use an intermediary instead.

It is easy to see many examples today of how the concept of *ma* continues to influence Japanese society.

When you have a serious matter to report or an important request to make, you do not act immediately but rather wait for a more appropriate time or use a third party to pass on the message.

Or when seeking to ease tensions with a friend or colleague, it is common to avoid the contentious subject entirely and leave some time before bringing it up. In this case, the Japanese say *sukoshi ma o oite* ("take a little break").

Even within a single conversation, the Japanese like to take breaks, allowing for periods of silence. It is evident that these silences can be uncomfortable for some non-Japanese; business books for Western negotiators often caution them against blathering on and spilling important information just to alleviate the awkward silences imposed by their Japanese counterparts.

It is not necessarily the case that the Japanese are being

devious here. They are simply used to long periods of silence, and that is probably because the concept of *ma* is at work.

moderation

中
庸

CHŪYŌ

Realizing that truth always lies somewhere between black and white allows you to see your own connectedness with others from a perspective of moderation.

The mindset that stays away from the extreme and always seeks out the middle road describes the concept of *chūyō*.

A Japanese organization maintains *wa* ("harmony") by enabling employees to work with each other in a balanced way that carefully takes all points of view into account before the best of the group's ideas is adopted as a course of action.

In Japan, a leader can thus sometimes be described as having a "modulating style." This expression describes a personality capable of managing by taking all relationships seriously and adjusting opinions outside of the mainstream to fit with the whole. The respect paid to such leaders reflects the value placed on the concept of *chūyō*.

The biggest advantage of *chūyō* may lie in its avoidance of risk. It was Aristotle, the source of much of Western philosophy, who said that the extreme is bad and that the moderate should be respected.

Of course this *chūyō* approach has its weaknesses, since it makes it almost impossible to exhibit strong leadership or to take full advantage of a person's individuality. And in a global age where speed is the priority, it is not clear whether this approach of not quickly making decisions—of taking the time to carefully consider the opinions of many people—fits.

So it may be necessary for us to figure out how to employ *chūyō* while at the same time taking action with some degree of speed. Needless to say, the most important factor here is day-to-day communication with people.

consensus

NEMAWASHI

Developing consensus is like planting a seed: take time to let it grow. Find a path that everyone can agree on, and above all respect everyone's point of view and what they bring to the discussion.

In order to preserve harmony (*wa*) when going "on the record" with an opinion, the Japanese will cautiously share information with others but only *after* carefully taking place and timing into account. A typical Japanese form of communicating one's intentions in this situation is *nemawashi* ("lobbying").

If you present a proposal for the first time right at a meeting, there is a risk your superiors or others affected by your idea may be against it or feel blindsided. To avoid this risk—and the awkwardness—you engage in *nemawashi* by consulting prior to the meeting with key persons and walking them through your proposal and adjusting it as needed to win their support.

If you have done a thorough job of *nemawashi*, there will be little opposition at the meeting and your proposal will be approved.

It is common for a *nemawashi* session to take place outside the office, perhaps over dinner or while playing golf or at some other private setting (*ba*).

Repetition of *nemawashi* will naturally result in fewer conflicts and more complete and regular sharing of plans and ideas.

The original meaning of the word *nemawashi* is "encircling the roots," or in other words, carefully digging a circle around the roots in order to preserve them when moving a plant or tree to a new location.

Similarly, when conducting *nemawashi* for a proposal, you are trying to carefully create a circle of consensus among the key people involved in order to move the proposal unscathed to the formal setting of a meeting.

Nemawashi is very common in Japanese organizations. It is important for non-Japanese to also move into "the circle of consensus" when conducting business in Japan by spending more time in *nemawashi* over drinks or in other informal settings.

People often think the Japanese are entirely governed by formal rules of behavior. But *nemawashi* shows just how important informal, one-on-one settings are in communicating in Japan.

flexible thinking

Society needs rules, but also flexibility and a willingness to bend the rules to the situation. The goal of any solution should be to satisfy human needs, and not to satisfy arbitrary guidelines.

The word *yūzū* is often used in business as a term related to the lending of money. But its original meaning suggests the ability to adapt flexibly according to the situation. The opposite of *yūzū* is *shakushi-jōgi*, which means to measure things precisely by a "dipper and ruler" in a rigid, Procrustean manner. *Shakushi-jōgi* is disdainfully used to indicate a way of thinking that doesn't allow any exceptions to the rules or any variations to what has already been decided.

The *yūzū* mentality, in contrast, doesn't see things as being either black or white but decides according to what is most appropriate to the occasion and acts in a way that the other party will find most satisfying. From olden times, *yūzū* has played a hidden role in the judicial system and promoted the smooth running of society. It has provided the psychological leeway to calm the nerves of those engaged in the fierce clashes and conflicts that occur in the legal world and in government bureaucracy.

On the debit side, when *yūzū* is misused, it can lead to organizational dysfunction and to the usurping of power for personal use by those with the authority to do so (as in the phrase, "the ends justify the means").

Many people these days lament that the concept of *yūzū* is slowly being lost. If the flexibility of *yūzū* disappears, the oil that lubricates society will disappear too, and along with it the spirit of consideration for the feelings of others and the ability to judge for oneself and make appropriate adjustments.

Follow Forms
and Paths

form

型

KATA

Japanese arts teach by having students imitate models. The willingness to copy traditional forms comes not from rigidity but from the modest belief that there is much to learn from past masters.

We have emphasized how *wa* ("harmony") has long been an essential social value in the communication style of Japan. Here we introduce *kata* ("form"), another core Japanese value that promotes social cooperation over individual thoughts or abilities.

In ancient times, people in agricultural communities gave thanks to the gods, creating various ceremonies that also helped to strengthen bonds between people. Later, in feudal times, as a class system developed, additional forms of etiquette and behavior came into being as a means of expressing the difference in rank between one person and another.

To ensure that all people would appropriately follow the various ceremonies and etiquette, the concept of *kata* developed, whereby a particular *kata*—that is, a prescribed form or sequence of doing something—would be followed at a particular place and time.

Nowadays, you can see *kata* in action in all aspects of Japanese life. The exchange of name cards, the pre-bout rituals of sumo, even the relatively mundane act of pouring and receiving a cup of *sake*—are all examples.

In *budō* ("martial arts") and in other traditional disciplines, the student's first goal is to cultivate the *kata* related to each activity. The more quickly you are able to master *kata*, the quicker you will advance to the next step. For the Japanese, before tackling a project, it is essential that they first understand the process by which that project will be completed. It is not proper to take random actions, trying to accomplish things through trial and error. Rather one must first understand the answer to the question: How?

The why is often not important at all. Ask many Japanese craftsmen and they will tell you that the "why" is embedded in the "how." The point of doing something properly, in other words, is to do it, and meaning flows from the extended mastery of technique.

etiquette

SAHŌ

Only by adhering to proper form can you enter a space that allows you to act freely and express your leanings and desires. In etiquette is found the beauty of mastery.

Sahō describes forms of behavior that have been established by society over a long period of time. During the feudal period in Japan there was a class system in place. Knowing how to behave toward a person of higher rank was of the utmost importance.

Sahō means doing what fits into the proper *kata* ("form"). Just as Westerners greet each other with a handshake, so do the Japanese have their accepted forms of behavior when they meet each other: the passing of the business card, the bow, the rote exchange of phrases of greeting.

Another example is seen in the tea ceremony, where every action is carefully choreographed, from where people sit, to how the water is boiled, to how the tea is prepared and served and sipped, and so on.

In the business world, one can observe *sahō* in action as the seller employs deliberately polite language and bows often as he shows various forms of respect to the buyer. Within the social setting of a company, a subordinate will use particular *sahō* with his boss throughout the day, in the form of language and tone of voice, deference at a meeting, locating his seat at a table, and so on.

These and many other forms of etiquette of the Japanese today reflect practices that have been in place for centuries. For most Japanese, *sahō* is an ingrained pattern of behavior that affects their day-to-day actions without them even being aware of it. For people who come from overseas, some of these behaviors may appear puzzling. Why is someone bowing so many times in one setting while sitting unnaturally ramrod straight in another? But for the Japanese, they are simply following the *sahō* that is appropriate for that place and circumstance. Even a rebellious Japanese youth with idiosyncratic leanings will know how to behave "properly" in just about any situation, and in almost all instances will do so if the situation requires.

discipline

SHŪREN

"How to do it" is not important. Knowing proper form and how to achieve it comes from understanding heart and meaning. Discipline builds both spirit and character.

When learning a new *kata* ("form"), a student will repeat the same action innumerable times, whether it is a *jūdō* throw or the strokes of a calligraphy brush or the steps of a dance. There is ultimately a logic to all *kata*, but in order to truly understand that logic the student must continue to silently repeat the action again and again and again.

The teacher does not tell the student why something must be done in a certain way; he simply continues to have the student repeat the action until he, the teacher, is satisfied. In Japan traditionally there is no culture of "feedback." The student trusts the teacher and follows the directions of the teacher without questioning.

In certain cases, swordmaking to name one, a student may find it necessary to spend many years in training to master the various *kata* of his art. Only then, after the *kata* have been mastered, does the student first understand the true logic of his movements, and then from there he may further develop his skill and permit his own originality and style to emerge.

This demanding process of learning a *kata* is called *shūren*. *Shūren* can be seen in the business world in the interaction between subordinate and boss. The new employee is expected to watch the boss and learn what to say and how to behave, and then, when finally given a task to perform, to repeat those behaviors with little hope of explanation or comment. In recent years the example of the Japanese boss who manages his subordinates harshly without any feedback has become rarer. But Westerners with Japanese bosses are still often puzzled by the lack of feedback, praise, or guidance.

skill

技

*Few people these days are apprenticed in
the old style. But if you truly want to learn
a skill, there is no better way than to find an expert teacher,
learn from close observation, and practice diligently.*

When a person repeats *shūren* to the extent that he is now able to teach others, it is said that he has truly mastered a *waza* ("skill").

The accomplishment is duly noted and respected, but the practitioner must continue to be modest and further "polish," *migaku*, his skills. The word *migaku* in this case comes from the act of polishing a sword, which a samurai would have to do to his weapon many times over in order to bring out its best.

When a person "polishes his skills," he is not simply improving technique; he should also expect to become stronger mentally and spiritually. Therefore a teacher will pose particularly difficult questions and topics to his best students, in order to toughen them up. The teacher, in a sense taking on the role of a parent, will go so far as to probe into the life of the student and in this way work to develop a well-rounded person as an equal part of the process of mastering a *waza*.

Even now, managers in companies may get involved in the personal lives of their subordinates, giving direction on matters not directly related to work. This comes from the traditional practice of how a teacher interacts with a student in order to master a *waza*.

The difference between *waza* and its English translation, "skill," lies precisely here. A "skill" is mastered with a specific practical objective in mind. A *waza* is a skill that embodies the repetition, mental toughness, and discipline that went into learning it.

craft

匠

TAKUMI

To reach a high level of skill you observe form, learn methods, and devote yourself to diligent practice. True craftsmanship emerges when spirit and technique become one within you.

In recent years, those involved in traditional handicrafts in Japan have gained a renewed appreciation and respect. In Japanese, these people are said to have a *takumi* ("craft").

These craftsmen develop their *takumi* through many years of mastering a *kata* ("form"), followed by further polishing of their *waza* ("skill"). The number of such craftsmen, whose traditional items can only be made by hand, has been dwindling in our age of continued industrialization and efficiency. However, as the products created by these crafts-men have come to be reevaluated in recent years, so also have the *takumi* these artisans possess.

And this is true across the board. In the automobile industry, for example, efforts are being made through trial and error to pass on to younger workers the grinding and other skills that require detailed handiwork and intuition.

Getting the next generation to truly embrace various *takumi* and *waza* is not easy. There is in particular the issue of whether or not younger people will accept the tradi-tional teacher-student relationship. Will they respect their teacher, entrusting their lives to him or her as they polish their *waza*, or will they simply work to master a narrow skill for a paycheck?

Only time will tell.

way, road

道
MICHI

There is a path for right living and a path for right learning. Japanese observe the "way" because it subsumes everything in spirit and action.

If *kata* ("form") is the actual know-how by which a skill is learned, then *michi* is the social and spiritual value by which that skill is further strengthened, with deep roots in Japanese culture.

The Chinese character for *michi* can also be read as *dō* (from the Chinese *dao*). In English, *michi* would be translated as "way" or "road," the path used by a person to walk or by a vehicle to travel. Both words "way" and "road" are often used in Western languages as metaphors for life. In Japan, too, the word *michi* (or *dō*) is used metaphorically for the process of learning various *kata* as one proceeds down the road of life, doing what one must to become a more virtuous person.

The Japanese will often use *michi* or *dō* when describing the type of life led by a person. For example, if someone is leading an immoral life, they will say that that person is *fudōtoku* ("not on the road of virtue"). Or when a person pushes his skill to the utmost and is on the cutting edge of a field, the Japanese say that he is "taking the road to its ultimate destination" (*michi o kiwameru*).

The pronunciation *dō* most often appears as a suffix on words when the Japanese are describing circumstances where they must learn or polish a skill: *kadō* (written with the characters for "flower" and "way") is the art of flower arrangement; *kendō* ("sword" and "way") is the martial art of fencing; *jūdō* ("flexible" and "way") is another martial art; and Shintō ("gods" and "way"—here pronounced *tō*) is the native religion of Japan.

The word "Way" is often capitalized in English to emphasize that the path chosen represents a formal commitment.

reason

DŌRI

The clarity of its truth and inherent structure is the philosophy behind the Way, the overarching concept that keeps you from the temptation to stray and offering an answer when you ask why.

The English translation for *dōri* would be "reason."

The Chinese character *ri* in *dōri* is also read as *kotowari* and means the "inherent proper structure" of things or, in other words, "reason," "logic," or "truth." By adding the character for *dō* ("way") to *ri*, we come up with *dōri*, meaning the proper "structure" of a person, with the concept of "reason" clearly expressed.

In keeping with their social values that they have cultivated since feudal times, the Japanese use the phrase *dōri ni kanatta* ("following reason") to describe the actions of a person who pays proper respect to his elders, teachers, or superiors.

In other words, it is not enough to simply put forth clever arguments; to be "correct," *dōri* requires that one must also have a moral backbone supporting one's words, that one's actions must bend toward ideas of what is "true" that have already been established in the past. Morality and reason in Japan thus have an inherent or foundational basis and are themselves a kind of "path" or "way" (*michi*). Because these are based on traditional values nurtured in Japan, they are not something one can expect other countries around the world to accept.

the way
of the warrior

BUSHIDŌ

Bushidō *means "the Way of the Warrior." Born in ancient times, it developed in the feudal era and still resides in the DNA of modern Japanese.*

The concept of *michi*, or *dō*, was expressed in its purest form by *bushi* ("warriors") during the feudal period in the way of life known as *bushidō*.

In his well-known book *Bushidō: The Soul of Japan*, the Meiji-period (1868–1912) philosopher and diplomat Nitobe Inazo made the argument that *bushidō* is to Japan as Christianity is to the West, in the sense that *bushidō* is the source of moral law in Japan, providing the basis for judging right and wrong.

Another expression for *bushi* is *samurai*, a word that has become better known in the West. The *bushi* fought with swords, and at times could be called on to protect their masters or villages or towns from enemies. The samurai were *bushi* who, in the feudal structure of the time, served their lords.

As with the knights of the West, the samurai swore allegiance to their lords and were prepared to sacrifice their lives in defense of him and his land. To fulfill their role, the samurai trained hard both physically and mentally to develop a fortitude that could withstand the constant threat of death. This way of viewing life and the actions that grew out of such a view formed the *dō* ("way") that the *bushi* traversed; hence the word *bushidō*.

In the pursuit of loyalty, the *bushi* were always concerned about what to learn and how to act. As persons of higher rank than others, what type of responsibilities and rules did the samurai have to keep in mind? *Bushidō* taught the importance of controlling individual desires, not fearing death, and leading a simple life of integrity as one protected one's lord. Samurai were thus expected to be taciturn, unswayed by events around them, able to remain calm and respond to danger at any time.

In today's business world in Japan this way of thinking can still be found, as duty to one's company comes before individual gain, and company employees take care of their assignments with few questions. It can also be seen in the way managers must take responsibility for the mistakes of their subordinates.

Many older Japanese are disappointed that the younger generation has fallen away from the principles of *bushidō*. Of course, even in the past, the reality of *bushidō* was not always aligned with the ideal.

self-denial

KOKKISHIN

The spirit of self-denial teaches you to be fully mindful as you follow the Way, eliminating distracting thoughts and loosing yourself of ego.

Within the tenets of *bushidō*, the most highly valued is the virtue of *kokkishin* ("self-denial"). *Kokkishin* means, through spiritual training, conquering desire, fear, and other emotions in order to overcome the self.

The Japanese have traditionally liked the word *doryoku* ("effort"). They tend to more highly value the effort put into the process than the result itself. This relates to how much *bushidō*-like effort has been put into work or studies in the spirit of *kokkishin*.

Those who put aside their own desires and benefits, working hard instead for the good of their organization or group, will be viewed more favorably than those who produce results that benefit them as individuals.

Today's business world is results-driven. Even in Japan there are no exceptions to this. But it is also true that in Japan's business culture, more so than in other countries, there is still more emphasis on and recognition of the value of effort for effort's sake.

In this way, *kokkishin* is related to the social value of *kenson* or *kenkyo* ("modesty"), where one constantly puts oneself below others and quietly strives to better oneself.

This posture often leads to misunderstandings between the Japanese business world, where a taciturn approach is valued, and the West, where people are expected to speak up for themselves and take the lead when necessary.

training

業

GYŌ

What is training? You adopt an attitude of self-denial, refine your spirit, work on your skills. Now and then you must clean and purify yourself as you continue forward, eyes firmly on the Way.

If you had to translate *gyō*, the closest word in English would probably be "training." But this is "training" in the sense of tasking yourself with the demanding responsibility of working hard day-to-day to cultivate your *kokkishin* ("self-denial").

Buddhist priests who seek enlightenment (*satori*) by performing rigorous and tough training deep in the mountains are said to be "conducting *gyō*" (*gyō o okonau*).

The *shūren* ("discipline") used by a student when learning *kata* ("forms") may be said to be a type of *gyō*. Robert Whiting, an American author, has written that Japanese baseball is in fact not a sport but a discipline, *yakyūdō* ("The Way of Baseball"), along the same lines as *kendō* or *jūdō*.

Whiting points out that Japanese players do not simply practice baseball; they also place emphasis on the spiritual side in their training—paying respect to the ball field by keeping it clean, being properly deferential to their seniors, and even going so far as to sit in meditation in Zen temples. It must have been very clear to Whiting that the players were employing a particularly Japanese form of training, *gyō*, in order to reach the top of their game.

In today's business world, many aspects of *gyō* are also used in the mental or spiritual training of workers, such as task repetition, section rotation, group exercises, and even sloganeering.

For the Japanese, *gyō* is an essential value in all training; it is an important aspect of the *michi* ("road") one travels in seeking to accomplish anything.

truth-seeking

GUDŌ

What is truth-seeking? Follow where your teacher leads and remain quiet. Never worry about how you may look foolish as you study and devote yourself to the Way. Finally, develop heart.

Training and studying hard to thoroughly master something is called *gudō* ("seeking the truth").

If *gyō* is defined as the act of training in order to find one's way (*michi*), then *gudō* is the sincere spirit employed in doing *gyō*.

For the Japanese, who highly value the concept of *michi*, there is a strong interest in how you discipline yourself as you work hard to find your way and reach your goal. As with *kokkishin* ("self-denial"), the true aesthetic of seeking one's way is seen in the process itself; the journey is its own destination, in other words.

Even if the results are not what were hoped for, people will positively judge the effort made in the process. It is precisely in the spirit of *gudō* that something more than mere results is expected. From the perspective of Westerners, who place a heavy emphasis on results in their business culture, the spirit of *gudō*, which places importance on process, must seem impractical.

From the Japanese perspective, the experience and improvement in spirit gained through the effort are more important than results. The thinking here is that even if the results are not good in one situation, you will be able to better handle future situations, thanks to the stronger spirit you have developed.

In *bushidō*, it was thought that if a warrior trained correctly to develop the proper spiritual power, the results would take care of themselves.

In other words, coming out ahead in a battle is nothing more than the result of the training that has been done in preparation.

Feel Ki,
Be Mindful
of Change

energy, spirit

KI

Ki is the unseen power that fills all of space, it is a person's disposition or the collective force of a gathering. When the spirit of ki is full it is a blessing. All living things are infused with ki.

Ki, a concept developed in ancient China, describes the movement of unseen energy in our world.

For example, let's imagine a meeting where a strong difference of opinion prevents the discussion from moving forward. A contentious if not paralyzing atmosphere envelops the conference room. That atmosphere is an example of one type of *ki*.

Or when you walk in a morning's clear air you feel refreshed. The invigorating mood of your surroundings is an example of another type of *ki*.

In other words, if you encounter good *ki*, you feel energetic and positive, while if you encounter bad *ki*, you feel poorly and lack energy both spiritually and physically.

Ki has been recognized in Japan since ancient times, and today it still has a huge influence on how the Japanese think and view things.

Ki changes depending on the time and place, as well as on the relationship of the people involved and the circumstances of their communication. *Ki* is also found in people's hearts; the Japanese believe that if a person is full of good *ki*, he will be fulfilled in both his work and his personal life.

In most cases, you should be able to change your *ki* through your own efforts. For example, if you feel that your *ki* is not good, then you should consider in concrete terms how to improve it. If a meeting is not progressing well, then you might consider taking a break to change the *ki* and generate better energy.

The concept of *ki* is not necessarily logical. People who are capable of gauging *ki* and handling it in an appropriate way are highly regarded. Earlier we discussed the concept of *kikubari* ("thoughtfulness"). This is an example of understanding the *ki* of the moment and being attuned to the needs of other people.

fighting spirit

KIGAI

Fighting spirit best emerges when ki *is full not just within you but sensed all around. That is when the "can do" attitude kicks in and makes you ready to fight.*

The phrase *yaru ki* describes the can-do attitude expected of a new participant in a group. *Kigai* is the strong and continuous daily expression of that will, a person's relentless fighting spirit.

It is common in Japan to highly value the praise of superiors and colleagues you earn through your *yaru ki* or *kigai*. Even if your results are not good, if you demonstrate *kigai* and are able to contribute good *ki* to the group, you will be favorably evaluated.

Conversely, if you do not show sufficient *yaru ki* or *kigai*, then no matter how well you do your work you will be treated as an "outlaw" and may not be promoted within the group.

This may be one of the reasons why group action is such a strong component of Japanese society.

In the same way that *ki* is based on atmosphere, not rational thought, there is no connection between *kigai* and business logic. An observer could say *kigai* is simply a matter of expressing enthusiasm, and that is probably true. But having enthusiasm is also an expression of love for and loyalty to one's group or organization. Most Japanese believe that the power of the group created by pulling together the *kigai* of everyone will produce better results than relying on individual performance.

fate

運気

UNKI

Ki and fate are intertwined. A person with a strong sense of ki, *like a forest, mountain, waterfall, or river, emanates strength from its presence. Grasping one's fate and approaching it with an attitude of self-denial is the key to success.*

The word *unki* refers to the practice of fortune telling. Like the astrology of the West, a method of predicting a person's fate based on a complex analysis of the stars or a birthdate or name has existed in China, Korea, and Japan since ancient times.

Fortune telling is popular in Japan; many people watch featured segments on TV shows or go to street stalls in the cities for palm reading and analysis of names.

Unki has a strong connection with the movement of *ki* ("energy"). When the *ki* is not good, your *unki* will be in a downward trend, and it is at such times that it is easy to become sick or run into trouble.

Ki is an energy that cannot be seen; it exists in individuals and also in relationship to the movement of the universe. People with strong control over their own destiny are those who are able to take hold of that *ki* and through their own efforts pull that energy into their lives.

In addition to the meaning of *ki* ("energy") introduced above, *ki* can also refer to feelings or state of mind. In Japanese the word for illness (*byōki*) is made up of the Chinese characters for "sick" (*byō*) and *ki*. If you are in a positive state of mind, you may be able to overcome an illness on your own and bring yourself good luck.

sensing danger

SAKKI

The mere sword wielder will reveal his hostility and be consumed in a murderous rage. But the true sword master will cloak his feelings in an air of serenity.

Sakki is another concept that helps in our understanding of *ki*.

In the old days, it was said that a well-trained samurai could sense someone's intent to kill him even before the opponent had drawn his sword. That foreboding in the air is what is known as *sakki* ("sensing danger"). In other words, even without words or clear actions (a curse or a glare, for example), the atmosphere and subtle facial expressions or movements would allow the accomplished samurai to read the *ki* of his opponent and make his mental preparations for a fight.

The *ki* you emit is sent to the person you are with, and that person in turn readies himself so that he can now send his message to you without using words. By exchanging *ki*, two people are thus able to express their wills to each other.

To the modern mind, this sounds like the stuff of comics or movies, but it is a fact that even today the Japanese expect to be able to express their feelings to others without using words. It is because of this that non-Japanese people are often puzzled and have a difficult time trying to understand what the Japanese are saying—or are not saying.

air, atmosphere

KŪKI

What is the goal? Without words you can pick it all up from demeanor and atmosphere. Ki is everywhere. Read the ki *and you'll understand.*

Kūki ("air") is not simply a physical phenomenon. In English as well, "air" is also used to describe the atmosphere of a situation.

In the Japanese phrase *kūki o yomu* ("reading the air"), the conditions that have brought about a particular atmosphere or situation are said to be the *kūki*.

The Chinese character *kū* in *kūki* is the character for "sky" and also means "empty." Combining it with the character *ki* ("energy" or "spirit") yields *kūki*, or "air." Put another way, *kūki* is not merely a physical phenomenon; it includes all of the various energies that permeate a particular situation.

As a strategy for making their way in life, the Japanese will first try to determine what particular energies (*ki*) are coming into play in a situation and will then try to take appropriate action based on that understanding.

The concept of *kūki* is therefore related to the concept of *ba* ("place"). The timing and combinations of when and where people get together will create various types of "atmosphere." For example, as part of your communication strategy in a meeting with your colleagues, you must decide whether or not to bring up a particular subject based on the *kūki* of a particular *ba* ("place").

Ki is the energy that is created by the interchange between people. Most Japanese feel it is important to understand the circumstances of the people around them in order to create good *ki*.

turning point

FUSHIME

Time passes. People change. Go with the flow and note the transitions. Like the joints on a bamboo, for good or bad people's lives have starts and stops.

For the Japanese, who place much weight on the values of *kata* ("form") and *michi* ("way"), it is important to always take note of milestones. In Japanese, the Chinese character *setsu*, also read as *fushi*, expresses this concept of marking a transition.

Setsu is, for example, used to make the word *kisetsu* ("season"), as the passage from one season to the next marks the passage of the year. The same character, this time read as *fushi*, is also the word used for a node in a bamboo stalk. The growth from node to node is what eventually results in a fully grown stalk. It is the same with one's life or with the process of learning: each period is important and builds on the previous; you cannot proceed to the next period without the last.

Thus we use the word *fushime* to indicate an important transition point in a person's life.

When seeking to master a skill, it is critical that continuity be preserved and that the beginning and end of each period be consciously recognized and connected with the preceding and following periods. This is inherent in the concept of *fushime*.

From the point of view of Westerners, it must sometimes seem that the Japanese are simply enacting superfluous ceremonies whenever they mark the end of a period by going to the trouble of making various greetings and thanking people, rather than just moving on. But for the Japanese it is a matter of making sure that the last *fushi* is properly cultivated, like the bamboo, in order to ensure the growth of the next.

The life value of *fushime* leads us to carefully consider what has happened in the past before moving on to something new.

restraint

SETSUDO

Satisfaction comes from not asking for much. By tamping down your own desires, you become able to preserve harmony and exchange a sense of gratitude with others.

Just as each node in a bamboo stalk is like each period in your life, so it is that you must do the utmost to train and prepare yourself at every stage, being careful not to go on to the next stage before you are ready. This virtue is called *setsudo* ("restraint"). On pages 20–21 we discussed the value of modesty (*kenjō*), and here we will see how modesty is reflected in the concept of *setsudo*.

Instead of your seeking individual recognition, *setsudo* means you work hard day-to-day to improve yourself within your current position and situation. Like a craftsman, you focus on getting each movement and action correct, confident that together they will form an auspicious whole.

This virtue, which has been cultivated in Japan since feudal times, may not fit with today's world, in which dynamic change is the norm.

Non-Japanese may often complain that they don't know what the Japanese are thinking or what they want to do. *Setsudo* may be behind this, as it may dissuade the Japanese from giving strong opinions.

On the other hand, *setsudo* tends to lead the Japanese to offer gratitude and respect to others.

In today's business world, the amount of teamwork that can be brought to bear on a project is very important. If an approach employing *setsudo* is used, in which the position of other people is carefully considered and proper respect is paid to them, then in a surprising number of cases it will be possible to change conflict into synergy.

The largest goals can be achieved by an accretion of small, manageable ambitions.

drawing a line

Take responsibility in all things and the ki will flow. Likewise, when you reach a turning point, face it with a concentrated attitude and your ki will be at rest.

KEJIME

Complementing the notion of *fushime* ("transition point") is *kejime*, the action a person takes when he or she decisively marks a significant change or development.

For example, if you commit a crime and, instead of running away, turn yourself into the police and submit to the appropriate punishment, this is called *kejime o tsukeru* ("drawing a line"). Having the right attitude that compels you to own up to and take responsibility for your actions is crucial here.

The Japanese today remain very committed to the concept of *kejime*.

For example, it is quite common in Japan for the chief executive of a company to resign if his company has manufactured and sold defective goods. Even if the CEO was not the direct cause of the defective goods, as the head of the company it is incumbent on him to "draw a line" (*kejime o tsukeru*) and take responsibility. For the Japanese, a person will be judged on how sincerely he "draws the line" during such a transition point in his life and in that of his organization.

temperance

SESSEI

Don't spend your time on useless endeavors or cultivate lavish appetites. Temperance is not being miserly or practicing self-denial but is a gentle means of getting through this life.

The word *setsuyaku* is used to describe the process of economizing on material things, like buying less and using what you have more efficiently. A related word, *sessei* ("moderation"), is the means by which aspects of the human mind and body are similarly used without waste.

In Japanese there is the phrase *hara hachi bu* ("80% of the stomach"); it means to avoid indulgence and instead eat with *sessei*.

Another Japanese saying admonishes us that "having too much is the same as not having enough." In other words, *sessei* means that one must always understand one's limits and live within them; *sessei* means living a life with an attitude of *setsudo* ("restraint").

Another Japanese phrase says, "know what is sufficient." This means your knowing what is enough to satisfy and not asking for more than that, living modestly within the circumstances of that particular period (*fushi*) of your life.

The flip side of using just enough is using too much and

being wasteful, a condition described by the expression *mottai-nai*. This may refer to wasting goods and resources as much as to devoting your life to pursuits not worthy of your abilities.

Sessei is thus a kind of compass for leading a life supported by this way of thinking. The ideal in a life of *sessei* is to maintain your *wa* ("harmony"), not creating friction with others, while at the same time strengthening yourself spiritually.

This way of thinking was evident in the ethical teachings of Japan's feudal period and can also be seen in Buddhist philosophy. Zen teaches the need to escape from the insular bubble that is yourself, controlling selfish desires and the ego.

Sessei is the imperative to include such thinking in our everyday lives.

Have Feelings, Be Loyal

feelings

人情

NINJŌ

*In a world governed by strict rules be sure
your thoughts are infused with your feelings,
especially when dealing with others less
fortunate than yourself.*

Emotions that you feel for others and that you express in a direct manner are called *ninjō* (written with the character *nin* for "person" and *jō* for "feelings"). *Ninjō* includes a willingness to embrace the love of all people without question and empathy for those you come into contact with who have not been so fortunate in their lives.

For example, if a court is trying a criminal, the judge may give a lighter sentence if the defendant committed the crime due to the unfortunate circumstances of his environment. Here, the judge has been moved by *ninjō* and people will applaud his decision.

This type of sympathetic turn is often seen in the period dramas known as *jidai geki* ("samurai tales"). When *ninjō* moves a person to be generous in making a business or public service decision, it is considered a good thing in Japan and, depending on the situation, the more generous the gesture the better.

It is difficult for most Japanese to accept the idea that "business is business" and separate their personal feelings from their decisions as managers. Business in principle should be—and often is—conducted based on ideas objectively exchanged that lead to logical judgments. But in Japan it is also common to conduct business on a "heart-to-heart basis," and this can often lead to fractured relationships and bad deals.

When faced with someone taking an opposing position, however, you do try to take *ninjō* into account and do what you can to accommodate that person.

obligation, duty

It is when you spurn established convention and follow your feelings that you experience suffering. Duty is not opposed to feeling but often stirs feelings into action.

GIRI

Giri is one of the most fundamental values in Japanese society. It is defined as the sense of responsibility and effort that go into maintaining a relationship between one person and another.

If you are indebted to another for a favor done, you are said to have *giri* to the other person. Japanese ethics require that you be well aware of the *giri* incurred and repay the favor.

In everyday life, an example of *giri* is giving gifts and making the rounds of greetings during the summer and at the end of the year to those you are indebted to for social or business favors. Another example, rare nowadays, is for subordinates in a company to help their boss move his household.

This type of connection from person to person has traditionally been strong in Japan. Especially during the feudal period, one's position was strictly fixed according to rank, sex, age, and so on. It was not possible to deviate from rank or make an attempt to better oneself within society.

Conflicts between one's obligations (*giri*) and one's feelings (*ninjō*) were thus a common theme in the traditional performing arts such as Kabuki or the Bunraku puppet theater. An example would be a daughter who became engaged to one man to fulfill her *giri* to her father, while her true affections (*ninjō*) were for another young man. This would be a classic *giri-ninjō* theme.

A more modern version of a *giri-ninjō* conflict would be when your boss invites you out for a drink on a night you already have a date set with your boyfriend or girlfriend.

Older people today are not so happy with the way younger people tend to put *ninjō* ahead of *giri*.

social debt

恩
ON

Obligation is born when someone does good for another. Japanese society is built on a foundation of social debts. Your debts can never be sold off, but are carried in the heart.

The social value known as *on* is closely related to the concept of *giri* ("obligation").

In the feudal period, a lord would pay a samurai in his service a sufficient stipend to guarantee his position in society. It was the usual practice to guarantee that rank not just to that particular samurai but to his descendants as well.

Having received a position and the guarantee of a living, the samurai would have incurred *on*, and in order to repay that social debt, he would loyally serve his lord, at times even put his life on the line. This fulfillment of his debt to his lord was the samurai's *giri*.

Even today, people often speak of "having *on*" to a particular person. Common examples are the *on* that is incurred by a child to his parent, or a student to his teacher, or an employee to his boss.

It is expected that those who incur *on* will make efforts to repay it. In most cases, *on* and *giri* attach to a relationship for a lifetime and not for the short term or to some specific circumstance in which the mutual obligation is fully discharged (unless, we suppose, one dies for one's lord). In the old days, forgetting to repay one's *on* was considered very unethical.

The concept of *on*, so deeply rooted in the character of the Japanese, is one reason many Japanese are not able to take a more "business-like" approach to business and instead allow personal feelings to affect their judgments. They choose to ignore, for example, the inequities that can result from giving favorable consideration in hiring or promotion to the child of someone to whom they have incurred *on*.

Still, it is a thing of beauty when someone reaches out to assist the child or other family members of a person to whom he has incurred *on* after that person has died.

insider / outsider

UCHI TO SOTO

Inside and Outside create the complex matrix of Japanese society. What you say openly to your group you hold back from others. And what is in compared to what is out is full of dynamic variation.

When a person is able to navigate the *shiga-rami* ("barriers") of a relationship and understand the particulars of *jō* ("feelings") versus *giri* ("obligation") to the point that you can let your guard down and truly trust that person, then it is said that that person is *uchi* ("inside").

In contrast, someone who is not within your family or close associates at your company is considered *soto* ("outside"), and you may have some reserve in dealing with them until you get to know them better.

How to distinguish between *uchi* and *soto* depends on the situation. For example, people in the same village who are not in the same family will be considered *soto* in terms of family, but those very same people will be considered *uchi* in terms of the village versus people from outside the village. It follows that if we take Japan to be *uchi* ("inside"), then foreign countries must be *soto* ("outside"). Thus, in Japanese a foreigner is literally called *soto no hito* or *gaijin* ("outside person").

To reduce the risk of dealing with the complications of relationships, the Japanese have traditionally tended to really open up to share information and personal feelings only with people who they felt were "inside" (*uchi*) their social circle. To be mutually welcomed as *uchi*, two persons must know each other well both publicly and privately. Then they will be in a position to express their feelings (*jō*) as persons who reside "inside" the same social circle and freely share information.

In the business world, Japanese will have dinner and drinks together as they attempt to build a relationship in which they can both be "inside." Foreigners are not expected (or welcomed) to break into the social circle, and they may continue to be treated politely as guests without ever being able to get their Japanese counterparts to open up to them.

true feelings and facade

本音と建前

HONNE TO TATEMAE

Were everyone just to speak their true feelings the harmony of society would be destroyed. So exercising discretion and restraint is actually a more sincere way of dealing with human relationships.

Two words most closely indicative of the relationship of *uchi* ("inside") and *soto* ("outside") are *honne* and *tatemae*. *Honne* refers to the true feelings that are spoken by those who are "inside" (*uchi*) the same group, while *tatemae* is what is spoken for show or to be diplomatic.

For those who understand the Japanese communication style, it is relatively easy to see the difference between what is *honne* and what is *tatemae*. However, it is quite common for non-Japanese people to hear what is *tatemae* and misunderstand it as *honne*, later being surprised when things don't progress as they had thought they would. As a result, the Japanese may be accused of being deliberately deceitful. At a meeting you might be told that the Japanese company is happy to consider all points of view when in fact its executives have clearly already made up their mind regarding their course of action.

In order to grasp the true intent (*honne*) of a Japanese person, you will be expected to become a member of his "inside" (*uchi*) group or go through someone who is already on the inside, like a colleague, classmate, or family member. Note that the insider who invites you "in" now bears some responsibility for whatever you do next, so simply asking to be let "inside" is often not enough. Getting to the point where others feel comfortable enough with you to share their *honne* and not just their bland *tatemae* requires additional time and effort.

good feelings

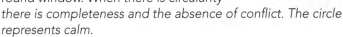

Japanese prefer circular shapes. There is something soothing and comforting at viewing foliage in a garden through a round window. When there is circularity

ENMAN

there is completeness and the absence of conflict. The circle represents calm.

Enman refers to a situation in which everyone's feelings are treated with mutual respect and harmony is preserved.

If a family is said to be *enman*, then we know that the relationships between the children and parents are good and that the whole family gets along well.

En means "circle" and *man* means "full up." The Japanese think of a round shape with no parts protruding as a state of *wa* ("harmony"). The phrase *subete ga maruku osamatta* (literally, "it's all settled into a circle") means that a solution to a problem has been found, and all of those concerned are satisfied.

The Japanese feel it is important to put feelings first, rather than logic, and they will often enthusiastically compromise to build the "harmony" (*enman*) of a relationship. So if a Westerner insists too much on putting his or his company's own needs first, this may disrupt the harmony and make a Japanese uncomfortable.

A phrase from Japan now known around the world is "the nail that protrudes will be hammered down." In other words, those who pursue a deviant way of thinking or overly independent behavior may find that their group will work to rein them in and enforce conformity.

While this approach promotes harmony, it can also result in a reluctance to take leadership as well as added effort before a consensus within the group is reached. Japanese are often praised for their achievements as a group and criticized for their lack of innovation.

loyalty

忠
CHŪ

A warrior in feudal times was taught to wholeheartedly devote himself to serving his lord. Such is the duty of one who receives on *from another.*

Let's briefly go back to our discussion of *on* ("social debt"; see page 65).

A person receives *on* from someone and in turn incurs *giri* (an "obligation").

Within the concept of *giri*, *chū* is the particular type of obligation incurred to someone of high rank or position—to respect and serve them because they grant you your livelihood and a social rank. *Chū* might in English be described as "loyalty." In the feudal period, when rank and position were more clearly defined than today, the ethical norms governing the behavior expected from a sense of *chū* were all the more emphasized.

In today's modern society, awareness of *chū* is not as strong as it once was. But Japanese people will still feel great loyalty to their company, teacher, or coach and from time to time sacrifice themselves by taking on undesirable assignments for the greater good.

hierarchy

JŌGE

Vestiges of a class system still exist in Japan. There are seniors and juniors, teachers and students, masters and acolytes. These are the hierarchies that are at the basis of Japanese social norms.

The concept of "higher" rank and "lower" rank strongly influences *chū* ("loyalty"). During the feudal period, there was a strict system of hierarchy. Society was split into four classes—samurai, farmer, craftsman, and merchant—with the samurai at the top and the merchant at the bottom. Within the samurai class were several additional distinctions of rank.

In Japan today, *jōge* ("hierarchy," a combination of the characters for "above" and "below") is still evident in the relationship between boss and subordinate, or between teacher and student. It is also still very much alive in such traditional disciplines as martial arts, flower arrangement, and the tea ceremony.

There may be *jōge* relationships in place between government agencies and private companies, and a *jōge* relationship clearly exists between large companies and their subcontractors.

In Japan, your language (the words you use, your tone of speech) and the way you interact will be distinctly different depending on whether you are "higher" or "lower" than the person you are addressing. For Westerners, too, the concept of hierarchy exists, and the way one Westerner greets another will differ to some degree depending on the status of the other. In principle, however, in the West people are treated as equals and the hierarchy-based differences in speech and behavior are not as obvious as they are in Japan, where *on* ("debt") and *giri* ("obligation") are lurking in the background of most human relations.

devotion

忠義

CHŪGI

A warrior risks every sort of privation, even death, to repay his lord's protection with devoted service. The life driven by loyalty has its own logic and exhibits its own aesthetic.

The term *hōkō* ("service") was used in a general way to refer to the actions a samurai would undertake to repay *on* ("social debt") to his lord; *chūgi* ("devotion") was the ethical driving force behind the *hōkō*.

Chūgi is at the root of everything to do with the samurai spirit; it is a basic value that required the samurai to overcome his fear of death in order to maintain his loyalty to his lord. In order to do this, the samurai would constantly undertake spiritual, military, and scholarly training.

There is a tale in Japan called *Chūshingura* with which all Japanese are familiar. Based on a true story from the early 1700s, the story begins with a certain lord brandishing a sword at court and wounding a high official who had been maltreating him. Despite the fact that the lord had been responding to the bullying of the official, he is ordered to commit *seppuku* (ritual suicide) by the government. His retainers, who have by his death become *rōnin* ("masterless samurai"), then carefully plan and execute the assassination of the high official. They succeed, and for this, the *rōnin* themselves are ordered to commit *seppuku*.

This action on the part of the *rōnin*, overcoming their fear of certain death in order to avenge their deceased lord, has been passed down over the years as an example of what is precisely meant by *chūgi*.

filial piety

孝

KŌ

In the castle you offer loyalty to your lord. At home you treat your parents with respect.
In society's hierarchy, the lesser venerates the greater, and those beholden to others serve them with respect.

During the feudal period, there was a strict *jōge* ("hierarchy") maintained between parent and child, with the father at the top overseeing the entire family.

Under these Confucian morals, children were expected to respect their parents and always give them due consideration. Children would even speak to their parents as if they were persons of different rank.

This type of attitude toward one's parents was called *kō* or *kōkō* ("filial piety").

Filial piety is a concept that exists not just in Japan but in many other countries, including Korea, where the influence of Confucian morals is strong.

The relationship today between parent and child has become much more casual. It is rare now to see actions taken based on the principles of *kō*. However, at schools and other places of learning, filial piety is still often used as an example of a strong social virtue that should continue to be respected.

obstructions

しがらみ

SHIGARAMI

Relationships can become entangled in Japan, but such social obstructions prevent people from acting for selfish reasons and instead encourage them to carefully consider the position of others.

Japan's vertical society, with its highly varied types of relationships—such as hierarchy, inside/outside, *on* vs. *giri*—is quite complicated and demands ongoing choices as to behavior and communication style. The Japanese call these types of complicated relationships *shigarami*, a word that originally referred to a device used to stop the flow of water. It took on a broader meaning in the sense that a person's freedom to act is restricted by the *giri* ("obligation") that he will incur.

In this way, the concept of *shigarami* is connected to all the ethical and moral considerations in Japanese society. A young couple dealing with the difficult conflict between *giri* and *ninjō* ("feelings") is an example of people typically caught in the *shigarami* of society.

That a special word *shigarami* even exists to refer to the difficulty of human relationships indicates how the common practices of an inflexible society have developed over a long period of time.

Revere the Gods and Buddhas

reverence

神
KAMI

Gods have since ancient times been thought to inhabit different objects and places. The Japanese kami is at the root of nature, a creative force residing in valleys and forests.

When Japanese refer to *kami*, they usually mean the gods of the Shintō religion.

Shintō has existed in Japan since early times but was instituted as a state religion for political purposes at the time of the Meiji Restoration of 1868, using the prestige of the emperor as its symbolic head. As a result, its beliefs and practices have sometimes been misunderstood.

At its roots, Shintō was a diffuse system of beliefs that developed over time in local areas throughout Japan and, like Hinduism, incorporated multiple gods. The followers of Shintō believed that the power of these gods resided in waterfalls, rocks, lakes, large trees, and other objects of nature. As an agricultural society, the Japanese would pray for an abundant harvest to the spirits represented by these natural phenomena; these religious rites were also an opportunity for the early Japanese to gather together to pray for the safety of their villages.

Throughout Asia, one can find religions that worship rocks and other objects in nature and that perform purifying rites with water. For the Japanese, who worshiped the mystery symbolized by nature, purifying one's body and soul before these natural objects was an important religious activity. Various types of ascetic training in the mountains developed and are even today rigorously practiced by wandering monks.

The native Shintō later mixed with elements of Buddhism from the Asian continent to help forge the spiritual values of the Japanese. This mixing of Shintō and Buddhist elements can be seen in such things as Shintō-like acts of purification during Buddhist trainings; it is also not uncommon to find a Shintō shrine right next to a Buddhist hall of worship.

In Christianity, people are expected to atone to a god for their sins. The appeal of Shintō for the Japanese is found in the respect paid to nature and, through being unified with the purity of nature, in turn becoming pure oneself.

purification

禊

MISOGI

Kami *reside in clear water and in sturdy trees and craggy cliffs. The world itself is* kami. *Therefore we keep our bodies clean and honor nature.*

The rite of purifying oneself before rocks, trees, and other objects of nature where spirits and gods (*kami*) reside is called *misogi*.

Misogi takes many different forms in the traditions of Japan. For example, throughout the country you can see people pouring water over themselves at festivals; or you might see people jumping into cold ocean waves on New Year's Day as they pray for good health in the coming year; or you might find people standing under a waterfall as part of spiritual training in the mountains.

The Japanese preference for taking a bath instead of a shower—soaping and cleaning themselves outside the tub before getting in—may be related to this custom of *misogi*.

People who participate in the rites of Shintō are expected to purify themselves with water and to always keep themselves clean. The act of *misogi* is not simply a matter of cleaning one's body; the Japanese believe it represents a cleansing of the soul.

For the Japanese of old, by first properly purifying the body and soul they marked the distinction between everyday life and the time spent before the gods. Even now, before entering a shrine to pray, Japanese will wash their hands and rinse out their mouths. Only after purifying himself will a Japanese pray to the gods for the welfare of his or her family or business.

defilement

KEGARE

Before the gods we clean ourselves, not just to be rid of defilement but to restore us to a state of innocence and purity—a condition that children come to naturally.

Closely related to *misogi* ("purification") is *kegare* ("defilement").

Kegare was not simply a matter of being physically unclean; it also referred to the wickedness in a person's soul.

Many countries have the traditional value of "purity" in their cultures. In Shintō, it is believed that the purity of children gives them spiritual powers lacking in adults, and traditionally, it was considered important that a woman remain pure (that is, a virgin) until her marriage.

Adults, who are no longer pure like children or virgins, will try to rid themselves of their *kegare* at shrines or other places of worship. A person must be purified before standing in front of the gods in order to not present a defiled self.

integrity

SEIREN

Shunning material desire, living a modest, frugal life . . . Many aspire to this state of mind, but in today's world how are integrity and purity achieved?

Seiren means to have a pure heart, with no personal ambitions. In the traditional Confucian philosophy of China and Japan, personal interests were put aside for the greater good of the public.

From Chinese comes the Japanese phrase *seiren keppaku* ("integrity and purity"), which means to ignore personal interests and act absolutely impartially, avoiding all dishonor and shame.

Confucian thought entered Japan early on, but it was particularly during the feudal period that the concepts of *on* ("social debt") and *hōkō* ("service") drove the importance of becoming a person of *seiren* ("integrity").

To this sense of "pure heart" was added the Shintō concept of *seiso* ("neatness"), and when these further mixed with the Buddhist values of Zen and the samurai values of *bushidō* there developed a way of thinking that prized simplicity and beauty. The ultimate artistic expression of this may be found in the minimalism of the Japanese rock garden.

A pure heart, clean and focused, in the moment, fiercely

determined—these are the ideals sought in most Japanese spiritual and cultural traditions.

japanese spirit

"Japanese spirit": words that should only have ever meant honoring obligations, integrity, honesty, and mindfulness were falsely interpreted and used to lead a nation into war.

YAMATO DAMASHII

During World War II, the phrase *yamato damashii* ("Japanese spirit") was abused by the militarists, whose exploitation of it inspired the Japanese people to fight on and sent many young men to their deaths.

Yamato is the ancient name of Japan. Originally, *yamato damashii* was deeply rooted in Shintō and referred to the spirit a person developed in purifying himself while being at one with the gods (*kami*) who resided in nature.

In the Meiji period (1868–1912), Shintō was made a state religion with the emperor at its head; with the growth of nationalism, *yamato damashii* came to mean the strong national spirit of the Japanese. Thereafter the phrase was used to enhance national pride. And then later, in the 1930s, *yamato damashii* was combined with the concepts of *chūgi* ("loyalty") and *messhi hōkō* ("self-sacrificing service") as the nation slid down the slippery slope into a totalitarian state and war.

Shintō is a religion unique to Japan. However, the roots of Shintō reveal that it has much in common with other animistic religions in the rest of Asia, as well as in Europe. *Yamato damashii* is an essential aspect of Japaneseness, and absent the taint of war it expresses the importance Japanese place on the spirit of Shintō.

buddhism

仏教
BUKKYŌ

The kami live in nature and have been manifest in Japan since ancient times. The Buddha lives in the human heart, and his teaching originated in India. These two strains of worship have fused within the Japanese people.

Buddhism (*bukkyō*, or "the teachings of the Buddha") came to Japan from China around the sixth century C.E. It became attached to the imperial court and the emperor and over time split into different sects and spread widely among the people, taking many forms.

In its early period, Buddhism was more directly associated with the Buddha himself; in later times, as more sects developed, Buddhism was repositioned more closely in association with the "gods" as a manner of belief that could help save people from their suffering.

In other words, Buddhism evolved from being primarily a meditative discipline, such as Zen, in which one sought enlightenment, to a more diverse belief system that included many sects more centered on chanting as a way of finding salvation in the next world.

As it took root, Buddhism also combined with the native religion of Japan, Shintō, to create Japan's unique form of Buddhism. In Shintō, there is not a strong connection to an afterlife; rather, the belief is in the elements of nature and in how those elements can benefit one in this life on earth. Births in Japan are largely celebrated by Shinto, while deaths, funerals, and the afterlife are generally the province of Buddhism.

It is interesting to note that although Buddhism originated in India and came to Japan from China, the Buddhism we see in Japan today is primarily a product of the religious beliefs of the Japanese.

self-power and other-power

自力と他力

JIRIKI TO TARIKI

Even if you move through the world with an attitude of independence you will occasionally stop to entrust yourself to others and see where things are going. People adopt both attitudes.

Seeking to deepen one's beliefs through self-discipline, as in Zen, is known as *jiriki* ("self-power").

Seeking salvation in the afterlife through chanting to the Amida Buddha is known as *tariki* ("other-power").

Tariki came from the grassroots movement of Mahayana Buddhism. Particularly during the Heian period (ca. eleventh century) in Japan, the creed of Amida spread, as the common poor and sick and those affected by war found its message of salvation through chanting appealing. By the sixteenth century, the number of people embracing these beliefs had grown to the point that they became a threat to those in power.

Sects that emphasized *jiriki* were more popular with the samurai ruling class. There were thus two main directions of

Buddhism in Japan: the Zen sect of *jiriki* and the Jōdoshū and Jōdoshinshū sects of *tariki*.

Even now, the words *jiriki* and *tariki* are used in conversation, apart from their religious origins. For example: "Rather than asking someone else, you must do the work on your own (*jiriki*)."

the other world

ANO YO

Fear of the afterlife acts as a corrective. Worries of this sort among Japanese are largely the result of Buddhist teachings having taken root.

The world after death in Buddhism, the afterlife, is called *ano yo* ("the other world") in colloquial speech. In the section on *inga* ("cause and effect"; see page 104), we discuss how people who conduct themselves well in this world will go to paradise in "the other world" and then be reborn in favorable circumstances.

As Buddhism changed with the times in Japan, this concept of "the other world" was emphasized more. It was in the afterlife that one could achieve salvation through *tariki* ("other power").

The existence of "the other world" acts almost as an insurance policy for salvation for those who suffer or fail in this world. In "the other world," a person continues to exist as a spirit after death. It is that spirit that is honored in Japan at funerals and other memorial ceremonies.

There are many ghost stories in Japan about spirits who continue to be bitter and obsessed with this world and are not able to go on to "the other world." For example, the spirit of a person who was murdered may go on to "the other world" only after the murderer has been executed or has been haunted into committing suicide.

When a person is finally able to rid himself of the bitterness and obsessions of this world, he is able to go to "the other world" of the Buddha, which is paradise. Going to "the other world" is called *jōbutsu* ("becoming a Buddha").

Buddhist notions of heaven and the afterlife are quite different from their Christian analogues, which involve the concepts of sin, atonement, and maintaining the soul in some essential, almost anthropomorphic incarnation.

pathos

もの
の
哀
れ

MONO NO AWARE

Buddhist thought provokes an emotionalism, a sense of sorrow at the transitory nature of man and nature within an unchanging and eternal universe. This feeling of mono no aware *is the wellspring of Japanese aesthetics.*

In facing death and dealing with the fleetingness of life, an element of sentimentalism has crept into Japanese Buddhism.

In its origins, Buddhism was both a religion and philosophy that dealt with the changing circumstances of humans and the universe, as people sought to return to their natural selves through self-reflection and the control of their desires.

When Buddhism came to Japan and was confronted by the conflicting realities of life in the middle ages, it evolved to meet the needs of those looking for salvation in the next world, and as it did so it became more prone to sentiment, which could be described as the buoying of understanding with a profound depth of feeling.

Cherry blossoms are one example of a natural object that provokes this sort of sentiment. They bloom for only a few days in early spring before being blown off the trees. The sad beauty seen in this transition from fullness to nonexistence is what is meant by the phrase *mono no aware*, often translated as "the sadness of things."

No one knows when they will die. In the olden days a person could die suddenly at any age. As with the sad (a common adjective used here is "bittersweet") beauty of the brief life of the cherry blossoms, so it is with the *mono no aware* of the brief life of humans.

Popular art in Japan can often fall into an abundance of sentiment that is excessive and manipulative. But in the finer arts, where the presentation is notably more subtle and refined, the bittersweet strain of *mono no aware* is inescapable, piercing, and resonant.

transience

MUJŌ

"The prosperous will always fall" is a truism, as are age, sickness, and death. The seemingly unchanging landscape is in fact teeming with change. Impermanence is a Buddhist outlook that breeds mono no aware.

Mono no aware ("pathos") is an aesthetic way of looking at things, and *mujō* ("transience") is its analogue in Buddhism.

All things are constantly changing, and all living things eventually die. All that is glorious will decay, and there is nothing that will be able to maintain its current form—that is the concept of *mujō*.

In a sense, this was the first sorrow that Buddha embraced, and it was from this point that he began his journey toward Nirvana.

The epic *Tale of the Heike* was spread throughout Japan in the middle ages by monks who sang while playing the *biwa* ("Japanese lute"). At the beginning of the tale, it is famously stated that "everything is ephemeral, nothing is constant." This is a real-world example of *mujō*, as the story tells of the decline of the once all-powerful Heike family at the hands of their chief rivals, the Genji. "The prosperous will always fall" is one of the themes of the story.

This period of prevalent warfare spread disruption throughout Japan, leaving many families in despair and confusion as they saw their familiar world disappear in death and destruction. In order to deal with the transience and pain of this life, religious sects centered around *tariki* ("other power") developed, using earnest chanting to the Amida Buddha to bring peace and salvation in the next life. The Japanese may be resigned to the transience of life, but they are still hopeful of a better world beyond this one.

enlightenment

SATORI

Resigned to the truth that all things are transitory and ceaseless changing, you pursue your craft to the highest level of perfection. Such a person can accept death peacefully. Perhaps that is what is meant by achieving satori.

Having understood that "everything is ephemeral, nothing is constant," you then seek enlightenment (*satori*). To do so, you rid yourself of your enmities and desires by identifying their source and breaking the chain of such shortcomings, thereby advancing to the land of the Buddha.

Followers of the *tariki* ("other power") sects believe that through earnest chanting they will induce Buddha to come down and take them to paradise.

Followers of the *jiriki* ("self-power") sects believe that through self-discipline and meditation they will find salvation.

At the head temple of the Tendai sect, on Mt. Hiei outside Kyoto, there is a rigorous regimen of training called *sennichi kaihōgyō* ("circling the mountains for one thousand days"). Over a thousand-day period, the supplicant walks between 30 and 80 kilometers a day around the Mt. Hiei and Kyoto areas. Starting on the seven hundredth day, there is a special period of seven-and-a-half days during which the supplicant must read the sutras while not drinking, eating, sleeping, or sitting; each night he must also go down to the floor of the valley to fetch water as an offering to the Fudō Myōō, one of the five Wisdom Kings and perhaps the most important Buddhist deity.

Those who complete this rigorous training are called *daiajari*, and as a reward they are allowed to walk inside the Kyoto Imperial Palace with their shoes on.

All followers of Buddhism have a desire to find *satori*. Some Japanese believe that *satori* can be achieved through action; others believe it comes about through meditation and quiet sitting.

zen

ZEN

Zen is a Buddhist school that uses meditation and question-answer deliberations as part of a daily corrective routine. Zen does not rely on salvation from without but on internal reflection to grapple with mujō.

The Japanese sect of Zen is one of the most widely accepted forms of Buddhism in the West.

Imported from China during the Kamakura period (ca. 1300), Zen spread rapidly throughout Japan through the efforts of two sects: the Rinzai, which emphasized the question-and-answer approach between teacher and disciple known as *kōan*, and the Sōtō, which emphasized the meditative approach known as *zazen*.

Zazen's meditation places more weight on self-discovery than it does on intercourse with the Buddha; this meditation became part of the daily routine of self-discipline and spiritual training for many in the samurai class.

Zen has also influenced Japanese culture in many different ways.

Temple architecture and spaces reflect Zen's emphasis on simplicity, and Zen sensibilities can also be seen in such things as rock-and-sand gardens, the tea ceremony, and the martial arts.

Zen could be argued to be somehow present in all of the Japanese values we have discussed to this point. In the way that silence is valued over talking, or in the way that one's own desires should be controlled, or in the way that people communicate with each other—in all these behaviors we can see how the basic native value of *wa* ("harmony") was developed in tandem with Zen.

Zen permeated the ethical value system of the ruling classes, eventually transcending the sect to become an integral part of everyday life in Japan.

worldly desires

BONNŌ

*The ordinary person is surrounded
by worldly temptations. Some seek
enlightenment to overcome desire. Some
revel in a life of style and entertainment.
Both are ways of dealing with fleeting impermanence.*

In Buddhism, the various desires that humans have are called *bonnō*.

It is said that there are 108 desires, including the desires for wealth, sex, drink, power, and so on. In the ceremony *joya no kane* ("New Year's Eve bell"), the temple bell is rung 108 times on the final night of the year in order to cleanse away the 108 desires.

Buddhism teaches that to end your suffering you must constantly overcome your desires. Buddha himself meditated for a long period, battling with his own desires before finally ending them and finding enlightenment or, in other words, reaching Nirvana.

The state of Nirvana is called *jakujō*, and its Chinese characters imply reaching a state of nothingness/loneliness and quiet.

In Japanese, the word *seijaku,* an inversion of the characters for *jakujō,* is used to mean "tranquility" or "silence."

The Japanese often use the word *bonnō* in everyday

conversation. "I have so many desires (*bonnō*)" means a person has worries or obsessions that are troubling him.

A Japanese, even one who is not ordinarily religious, may seek to right himself through self-reflection, perhaps worshiping at temples in Kyoto or going on a lengthy pilgrimage and making the rounds of the eighty-eight temples in Shikoku. Japanese are awash in material desire, but their culture and traditions have provided them with established outlets for exploring modes of detachment and self-reflection.

emptiness

空
KŪ

Kū is emptiness, and when your spirit embraces emptiness it achieves a state of nothingness. The absence of material desire is naturally mirrored in the heart, and emptiness is projected onto all creation.

In the earlier discussion of *kūki* ("air" or "empty"; see page 53), we touched on the meaning of the Chinese character *kū*. Here let's look at the Buddhist implications of the character.

Kū denotes a state of nothingness, of being completely empty. In Japanese the word *kokū* also means a state of nothingness, but implies nothingness in a very minute sense.

One is able to find one's Buddha nature by shrinking down and ridding oneself of one's ego, the source of worldly desires.

Going beyond the already extremely small size of *kokū*, one continues to shrink one's ego ad infinitum until reaching the nothingness of Nirvana (*nehan-jakujō*). Interestingly, this same word is used in East Asia as a unit of mathematical measurement, while it also denotes the state of tranquility one reaches in enlightenment.

In today's materialistic society, people try to find spiritual freedom through an affluent life and the satisfaction of their desires. *Kū* is the complete opposite of this: the more you seek to attain your desires, the less your sense of fulfillment.

Japan is a capitalist country whose citizens are able to satisfy most of their materialistic cravings. Despite their economic attainments, many Japanese are spiritually exhausted.

Deep in their hearts, many Japanese want to experience the fulfillment and beauty of *kū*. Perhaps these are the ones who can feel completely at ease when they experience the simplicity of a rock-and-sand garden.

nothingness

無

MU

It is easy to believe that mu *and true enlightenment are the same. But the calm heart is easily rippled and befuddled by worldly desire. And many believe that* mu *is just another kind of aspiration.*

Mu ("nothingness") is similar to the concept of *kū*.

In Buddhism, there are no absolutes, and all effects have causes. Because there is no effect if there is no cause, there are therefore no worries if there is no desire. Going beyond the relation of cause and effect to find enlightenment (*satori*) in nothingness (*mu*) is one of the basic concepts of Buddhism. This philosophy, this way of looking at things, has had a huge influence on Japanese behavior.

The starting point for reaching *mu* is to look at things in a comparative and objective way. To do so, begin by taking the point of view of other people rather than your own, and from here you will first understand the connection between cause and effect in human relations.

For the Japanese, who place such importance on *wa* ("harmony"), this is an easy concept to accept. The principle of controlling one's desires and respecting the intent of others meshes well with the concept of *mu* to achieve an effective communication style for the Japanese.

This attitude is a strong characteristic of Japanese

conversational style and reflects a sense of reserve (*enryo*). This taciturn approach often leads to misunderstandings with Westerners, who tend to voice their opinions to express what they perceive as absolutely true and logically correct without first exploring what is true and correct about their environment at that precise moment in time.

In the concept of *mu*, one has no center in oneself. In other words, the desires of others are always central, not your own.

Taking yourself to the ultimate state of *mu* puts you in an ideal condition of tranquility, which in turn allows you to connect to others unselfishly.

Honor
Relationships

relationships

EN 緑

People come and go, but sometimes you wonder: Why is this person here? Is it by chance or some kind of destiny? Yet as your relationship deepens, what may have begun by chance turns inevitable and necessary.

En describes the concept of a relationship, from first meeting to farewell, and the bond that is developed therein.

The word *en* is also used in Buddhism for the relationships that are created by the Buddha as he brings one person together with another.

There is a phrase in Japanese: "even a chance encounter is preordained." In other words, all relationships have significance and must be nurtured. The ideal is to treat each person with respect and to make the utmost effort to maintain *wa* ("harmony").

In today's global business culture, nurturing personal relationships is more difficult when so much can be done remotely with email and videoconferencing. Yet the Japanese continue to place a great deal of importance on human interaction that develops *en*. They emphasize getting to know their partners and colleagues by eating and drinking together and—on occasion—sharing personal details.

Japanese also believe that if a person treats others well,

that goodwill will return to him in the future of this life or in a life yet to come. *En*, the connection between people, is thus for the Japanese a moral concept, grown out of Buddhist ethics.

reincarnation

輪廻

RINNE

After they die, do people go on to dwell in the afterlife? Who knows if there is truly a cycle of death and rebirth? But people do live on in our hearts, and many believe that through good deeds they will find themselves reincarnated.

The concept in Buddhism known as *rinne* ("reincarnation") teaches that all living things follow the laws of the universe and the Buddha, that they are born into this world in one form, die, and are then reborn in another form in a neverending cycle.

Rinne is the transition of life that links the past with the future, giving each person the hope that he will be happy in his next life.

In present-day Japan, there may be few people who believe in the literal truth of *rinne*. But it is not true that the Japanese do not believe in a future life. Many continue to hold a vague belief that one's spirit is present after death and that that spirit remains near its descendants, protecting them from evil and misfortune. Or they have the expectation that good deeds they do in this life will be rewarded in a future existence.

The concept of *rinne* can also be seen in festivals and Buddhist ceremonies where the dead are honored and their spirits treated with respect.

cause and effect

INGA

Evildoers must be punished. So say those charged with maintaining order in society. But standards of value are mujō—transitory in nature—and change with the times.

Inga expresses the Buddhist belief that for every cause there is an effect.

Related to *inga* is the often-used phrase *inga ōhō* (equivalent to "as a man sows, so shall he reap").

As we saw in the preceding section on *rinne* ("reincarnation"), the good or bad that a person does in a past life will determine his fate in the next life; in other words, the causes of the last life produce the effects in the next. This is *inga*.

The concept expressed by *inga ōhō* is not limited to the cause and effect of a past life on the present; the deeds you do today will also echo back to affect your fate in this life later on. For example, if you do not take proper care of your parents, you may not receive proper care from your own children.

Another case of *inga ōhō* would be committing a crime and escaping, but later becoming painfully ill and dying.

The concept of *inga ōhō* teaches that there is always an earlier cause for the difficulties or pains that a person may be suffering now.

By cultivating *en* ("relationship") with another, the Japanese believe they are not only attending to the present but creating a reservoir of good will of benefit to them and their souls for eternity.

disconnection

MUEN

Human connections are vital. But relationships can get sticky and produce all sorts of complications. A person can achieve a certain sense of isolation only by being strong enough to avoid entanglements.

Recently in Japan there has been much talk about *muen shi*, "death without ties"; it is used when discussing older people who have lost their connections to family and society and who die alone.

For the Japanese, who place such a priority on maintaining *wa* ("harmony") within a group, an isolated life following the dissolution and disappearance of all human connections may be the one thing they fear most.

Today Japan is facing a new reality, where the number of older people living alone is increasing and thus so is the number of people who die alone, away from their families. While the Japanese still place huge importance on connections to organizations and groups like companies and teams, the bond with family, which had been such a striking feature of Japanese society, continues to weaken.

Especially among younger Japanese, individual needs are more and more being placed before the needs of the society as a whole. Women are marrying later or not at all. Children are looking forward to an independent life, perhaps a career abroad. Who will look after the elderly today, and, decades from now, who will look after all those couples who have decided to forgo creating a family in return for fewer responsibilities and more disposable income?

The phenomenon of "disconnectedness" (a possible translation of *muen*) may not be considered a societal value as such. However, the increasing number of people who experience disconnectedness is one indication of how some of the basic values of Japanese society—many of them as old as Buddhism—are changing.

Build
Trust

trust

SHIN

How one demonstrates reliability varies depending on culture and country, and it's not easy for outsiders to judge good vs. bad. In the end, whether you decide to trust or not probably depends on who you are and where you live.

Shin refers to the strong and stable bond, based on mutual trust, that is established between two or more people.

In the Chinese character for *shin*, the element on the left side means "person," while the element on the right side means "speak." This implies that the words exchanged between people become the promises that produce a strong, trusting relationship.

Trust can be gained in different ways. Americans try to gain trust by looking directly into the other person's eyes and making a strong handshake. Americans believe that the clear gaze reveals sincerity and openness; the handshake is a ritual gesture thought originally to demonstrate the absence of a weapon

In Japan, in contrast, trust is gained by being modest and not putting one's own desires first, by being sensitive to the other person's position and speaking in a formulaic and indirect manner, and by not looking into the other person's eyes too aggressively.

Both cultures have ways of expressing trust that are in fact completely the opposite of each other. This can be a dangerous thing.

benevolence

仁

"Benevolence" is written with characters showing "two people." So benevolence represents consideration for others. It holds society together and is at the foundation of our world.

On the left side of the Chinese character for *jin* ("benevolence") is the element for "person," while on the right side is the element for "two." When two people come together, each person is necessarily aware of the other, and this awareness shapes their behavior. From this the phenomenon we call "society" begins.

The ideal of interactions between people based on the mutual sharing of knowledge and love came to Japan from China early on (ca. twelfth century) as one of the basic tenets of Confucianism. In order to maintain stability throughout the country, people believed that those above were respected, those below were cherished, filial piety was observed in the home with one's parents, and one's neighbors were treated with consideration and respect. *Jin* represents the virtue underlying these actions. Confucianism subsequently came to have a large influence on the ethics of all Japanese. Those who lived their lives in keeping with the practices of *jin* were respected as people who could be trusted.

There is a famous Confucian saying : "The man of flowery speech knows little about benevolence." What this means is that the more skilled a person is in verbal flourishes, the less sincere he is in his heart about the needs and feelings of others.

Once again we can see how the Japanese penchant for keeping a taciturn demeanor has been influenced by social practices many centuries old.

moral code

JINGI

The moral code of devotion may be obscured by its gangster embrace. But in human interactions, isn't saying that you have given your all to support another needed now more than ever?

A person of benevolence (*jin*) must honor one's *gi* or *giri* ("obligation"; see page 63). *Jingi* is the moral value that exhorts the individual to honor his promises because it is the right thing to do.

Among the common people, *jingi* is interpreted as the promises kept among friends or the *on* ("social debt") that is incurred with someone. *Jingi* is an especially important value for the gangster clans known as the yakuza in Japan, and there are many movies made whose central theme is the complications that arise from the mutual obligations shared by a yakuza boss and his underlings.

Put another way, to honor your moral code (*jingi*) is to engender trust (*shin*), and trust in turn strengthens your commitment to your moral code.

You will never betray those who are in your inner circle (*uchi*) if you have *jingi*. Having *jingi* means that you also have affection (*jō*) for those with whom you interact.

Chūgi ("devotion"; see page 73) operated in a similar fashion as *jingi* for the upper classes and samurai.

Develop
Virtue

virtue

徳

Those who respectfully listen to and counsel others are considered virtuous. And keeping your heart open to others who may be hasty or clumsy is a virtuous act.

The concept of *toku* ("virtue") carries a particular connotation in Japan, for by developing *toku* one learns what is necessary to be wise.

People of virtue are respected. Others will seek out their opinion or ask that they serve as a mentor.

What type of a person would a Japanese describe as virtuous?

First, such a person is *kenjō* ("modest"), never seeking to blindly promote his own interests. He also has a good understanding of *jō* ("feelings") and *giri* ("obligation").

Furthermore, such a person may have the *takumi* ("skill") to "take the road (*michi*) as far as it will go." But this person may have already reached a point where he is confident and settled, and is neither bitter nor naive about life.

A virtuous person has mastered life and knows how to adjust to its twists and turns. He is also a master at being able to enjoy life, following proper etiquette with grace while maintaining an ethical spirit. Being able to integrate wisdom with principle—this is the definition of *toku*.

shame

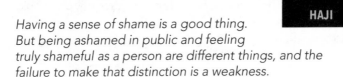

HAJI

*Having a sense of shame is a good thing.
But being ashamed in public and feeling
truly shameful as a person are different things, and the
failure to make that distinction is a weakness.*

Haji ("shame") is the flip side of *na* ("name"). *Haji* results not simply from doing something embarrassing; it involves staining one's name and thereby losing one's honor.

Westerners who are Christians will view an act that is contrary to the ethics of their moral law as a sin. Rather than sin, the Japanese are concerned with *haji*.

A person feels a sense of shame within, but *haji* also has to do with how you are viewed by the surrounding community. You can avoid *haji* by maintaining balance with others, seeking to avoid making a mistake that will put you at odds with your neighbors.

For example, if during a battle a soldier were to desert his unit out of fear, he would not only have to come to terms with himself about his shameful act, but he would also have to deal with the *haji* he had brought on his family, his comrades, his country, and if he were a samurai, the lord he was serving.

The ramifications of *haji* are vast. Under Confucian thought, the stain of *haji* extends to one's grandparents and even to one's grandchildren.

Most likely due to the importance placed on maintaining *wa* ("harmony"), the Japanese always tend to be concerned about what others will think. Whenever the Japanese do something different from what most other people would do, even if it is not significantly different, they must find the inner courage to battle and overcome their feelings of *haji*.

face

MENBOKU

When Japanese have a sense of shame they are more concerned with how they will appear to others. Having a clean public face is your most valuable commodity.

We often hear that the Chinese place a great deal of importance on "face." The expression "save face" is used when a person's position is protected and nothing is done to harm his social standing.

The Japanese have a similar concept of "face" (*menboku* or *mentsu*). You must always "protect your face" (*menboku o tamotsu*) by safeguarding your honor and making sure that your name does not become stained with *haji* ("shame").

A Japanese person will feel shame if he loses face, and he will be angry with whoever has caused it to happen.

For example, if you were to openly oppose your boss during a meeting, your boss would lose face because you are undermining his status. In order to avoid this, you will instead seek a different *ba* ("place") to present your objections. Your boss may in fact welcome disagreement, but he may not be able to accept any of your solutions if you present them publicly.

Menboku is thus closely related to the concepts of *wa* ("harmony"), *ba* ("place"), and *ma* ("space"). It conflicts sharply with the norms of most Westerners, for whom voicing one's opinion in front of others is not a bad thing and is even encouraged.

The Japanese always consider the position of others and ensure that no *haji* ("shame") is brought to anyone involved. By keeping the feelings of others in mind, *menboku* ("face") will be saved without making any special efforts, and *wa* ("harmony") will be maintained.

Japanese people are regularly complimented for being polite and agreeable. But how much of this is simply knowing what not to say and when not to say it?

role

BUN

Understanding your role is when you accept your status and operate only in the domain you've been granted. That was the rule in the past and even now many are resigned to such thinking.

The principle of *bun* concerns the "role" a person is expected to play based on his position in society. In the old days, it was taboo for a person of low rank to approach or talk to a person of high rank. This was known as *bun o wakimaeru* ("understanding one's role") and such practices were strictly enforced.

Today the principle of *bun* is still commonly found in the *jōge* ("hierarchy") relationships that one maintains according to one's social position.

A young person just joining a company will play his *bun* by respecting his *senpai* ("seniors") and obediently following their directions in learning his job. In clubs at school, the newer, more junior students will use polite language toward the older, more senior students—and also do menial chores, such as cleaning up after them. In department stores, door greeters and elevator operators will don servile uniforms and bow obsequiously to honored customers.

A person who does not properly play his *bun* may "do damage" to the "face" of another.

It is surprising that this concept of *bun*, typical of a classical "vertical society," is still alive in the hearts of Japanese.

In today's society, all people are expected to be treated equally, but the implicit mutual consent behind the concept of *bun* does contribute to the overall *wa* ("harmony") sought by companies and other organizations.

Those who are juniors today are seniors tomorrow, so the person who is patient and plays his *bun* to maintain *wa* knows that at some point his forbearance and diligence will be rewarded.

intuitive understanding

AUN NO KOKYŪ

Clustered on their narrow islands, people of the same land and ethnicity are alert to context and can read each other and communicate almost wordlessly, like "breathing in harmony."

One possible result of their shared social values is that the Japanese can get their point across with a limited number of words. This is known as *aun no kokyū* (literally, "breathing in harmony").

If you understand the position of the person you are dealing with, and if you are able to properly play your *bun* ("role"), then you will be able to control the flow of conversation in that particular setting, and it will not be necessary for you to use many words to do so.

There is no need to ask detailed questions about what is happening when you already grasp the spirit of *wa* ("harmony") and the *kata* ("form") required for that place and time. Wordlessly, your intent is immediately understood by the other person, and just by sharing the same space you are effectively "breathing in harmony."

Studies done in the past show that, compared to Westerners, the Japanese are able to infer meanings based on context more easily. This can lead to misunderstandings on the part of non-Japanese who, removed from the cultural context, cannot "fill in the blanks."

resignation

蹄
観

TEIKAN

Japan has a centuries-old tradition of roles and hierarchies that let you know exactly where you stand in the scheme of things. That can be good or bad, depending on how you take it.

From ancient times, *bun* ("role") has been closely related to rank and *jōge* ("hierarchy") relationships. In *jōge* terms , the rank above humans would be a god or gods, the cosmos, or something else beyond human knowledge.

Humans have a *bun* ("role") to play even in relation to that which transcends humanity. For example, humans cannot overcome death. Humans cannot see the future or change the past.

People who understand these limits in a profound sense—as the *bun* to be played by humans—may be considered wise; in other words, they are persons of virtue (*toku*).

The particular virtue here is known as *teikan*. The word means "resignation," but what *teikan* truly means is the wisdom of understanding human limitations and discovering what one's *bun* ("role") should be within them.

The ambitious seek to always press forward toward new objectives, but one of the virtues of *teikan* is that we try to treat other people better, which may come from our understanding that we all share the same limited space for the same limited time. *Teikan*, in other words, breeds empathy, not despair.

Appreciate
Beauty

beauty

美

BI

*Is the Japanese aesthetic sense unique or is
it like those found in other countries? If it is
unique, then it is fair to say that there are as many aesthetic
sensibilities as there are cultures.*

What is beauty (*bi*) for the Japanese?

For one thing, the ebb and flow of the four seasons is
very important. Geographically located in a temperate zone
of the earth, Japan is a country where summer, fall, winter,
and spring can all be experienced to their fullest. Each season has its own art, its own crafts, and certainly its own food,
each of which reflects the nuances of that particular time of
the year.

There is also the Buddhist element of *mujō* ("transience";
see page 90), which adds to the sense of impermanence seen
in the changing of the seasons. This theme is a common one
in classical Japanese literature.

The Japanese especially like to express their sense of the
seasons visually and indirectly. In many Japanese decorative
arts, conventional and schematized patterns and motifs or
other symbolic renderings are used instead of direct-from-
nature sketches. For example, in depicting a fall scene, an
artist may be able to make a deeper impact by drawing the
fine lines of colorful leaves arranged in a prescribed pattern

rather than a broader scene of mountains and fields. This type of indirect expression and the minimalism associated with it are particular features of Japanese art. They can be seen in the early gardens of Zen temples, in the lines and colors of woodblock prints, in the short, seventeen-syllable form of poetry known as *haiku*, and even in manga and anime.

the beauty of the common

わび

WABI

The Japanese favor the simple and rustic, like the picture of persimmons hung to dry from farmhouse eaves. Wabi *conjures up solitude and solace and describes an almost archetypal setting in the Japanese imagination.*

Wabi is the rustic beauty found in the simple and desolate, as opposed to the beauty found in bright and energetic colors.

Wabi is an aesthetic concept that began to emerge as part of the tea ceremony in the fifteenth century. Over time it spread across Japan not merely as applied to the simplicity of the tea house or the implements of tea but more broadly in connection with the Zen philosophy of meditation: in the process of existence, things are born with flaws, and over time they change. Wealth and materiality are fleeting.

Wabi dictates that rather than drinking *sake* from a cup elaborately inlaid with jewels, it is more refined to drink spring water from an unglazed bowl. *Wabi* is felt, too, when one is alone, surrounded by nature, observing the changing of the seasons and sensing the transience of this life.

the beauty of decay

SABI

We accept that there is no constancy, that everything settles into age, transition, and ultimately decay. Sabi takes the unending dance of motion and change beween man and nature and finds it a thing of beauty.

Sabi is the beauty found in that which is old and decaying. It is often linked with the concept of *wabi*, since rusticity and poverty are associated with buildings or furnishings that have seen better days.

You might, for example, see *sabi* in the worn grain of the polished wood of the corridors of an old Japanese house. And if you were to live in such a house, you would experience *sabi* (or both *wabi* and *sabi*) in the sounds of the night shutters being opened or closed, and hearing those sounds, you might recall the cold of the winter and be moved to self-reflection or to write a poem.

In Japan, people can be seen praying to old statues of the Buddha where the lacquer has fallen off and only bare wood remains. If there were no such appreciation of the beauty of their decaying appearance, these old statues would surely be repainted and restored to their original state.

Wabi and *sabi* are not simply the appreciation of the simple or the old; they also represent the conscious refinement of such elements into the realm of "beauty."

Moss is commonly used in Japanese gardens. *Sabi* is expressed by using moss-covered rocks in the garden: the growth of moss can only happen over a long period of time and in an area that is relatively undisturbed, while the rocks themselves embody the natural forces of the earth, seemingly permanent but in fact weathered and slowly eroding.

polish, refinement

艶

TSUYA

Tsuya *is a city aesthetic but not of the high-class sort. It celebrates a style of life and expression that is both casual and unharnessed.*

The word *tsuya* means "polished" or "refined." As was mentioned in the discussion of *wabi* and *sabi*, it is not considered refined to dress up in luxurious and glittering clothing. As *wabi* and *sabi* ideals came to reflect the tastes of high-class city people (mostly wealthy merchants), over time this "non-luxurious" stylish *tsuya* became a part of the sense of beauty held by the common people.

During the Edo period (1603–1867), activities in the licensed districts (that is, the pleasure quarters, distinct parts of town with brothels and other entertainments) had a huge influence on what was considered *tsuya*. Woodblock prints (*ukiyoe*) of dandies with the women of these districts became popular, setting the tone for fashion and other aspects of the daily life of the townspeople.

At this time, the city authorities used regulations to enforce a frugal lifestyle, and there were many restrictions on ostentatious displays of wealth. The townspeople were thus forced to adopt more subtle expressions of luxury and fashion, using but an accent here or there in their attire, or even in their underclothing, which could not be seen.

It may be said that *tsuya* combined the concepts of *wabi* and *sabi* with the townspeople's innate love of the flashy to produce a big-city sense of beauty. A refined person was considered both fashionable and sexy.

elegance

MIYABI

Miyabi is the aesthetic seen at ceremonies undertaken by the old imperial court and that of the capital Kyoto: an air of utter refinement coupled with splendor and elegance.

Over more than a millennium, the culture of Japan's imperial court developed a graceful style of elegance that in Japanese is called *miyabi*.

The culture of *miyabi* fostered by the nobles at the court in Kyoto predated and was in direct contrast to the "polished" culture of *tsuya* of the common people of Edo and Osaka, represented in their woodblock prints (*ukiyoe*) showing the popular fashions and entertainments of the pleasure quarters.

During the latter half of the fifteenth century and into the sixteenth century, Japan was in a period of almost constant war. The central government in Kyoto went into decline, and the *daimyo* (regional lords) came to dominate the politics of the country. In their quest for power, the *daimyo* sought to bring into their own domains the culture of Kyoto, and it was through this process that the *miyabi* aesthetic spread throughout Japan.

Today's imperial court is located in Tokyo and is largely ceremonial. But the elegant sense of beauty found in the earlier Kyoto court ideal of *miyabi* has not disappeared. It forms another strain of the Japanese aesthetic: subdued, sophisticated, studiously tasteful and mannered, rich with allusion to classics and clean of whatever is vulgar and common. Dyeing and pottery and other handicrafts of Kyoto spread throughout the country and today continue to be strongly rooted in local communities.

eroticism

色

IRO

The erotic in Japanese art may not be the same as "eroticism." It is not directly about sexuality but teases with an alluring and delicate, even elegant, appeal.

Except for the prudish Confucian attitudes of the samurai, the Japanese have in general tended to be open-minded about sex.

In Japanese, the word *iro* means "color" but is also used as a shorthand for love, sex, and the erotic.

The Japanese of the Edo period liked their sex scandals as much as people do today, and these were often used as the subject matter for the Kabuki or Bunraku (puppet) dramas. The government tried to regulate and restrict such risqué dramas, but loopholes were inevitably found and productions continued to flourish.

Iro is also frequently seen as an element of the Edo *tsuya* ("polished, refined") style, as part of the drinking and nightlife culture of the big city.

The genre of woodblock prints (*ukiyoe*) known as *shunga* were essentially the pornography of the Edo period. They feature men with outsize members and intense scenes of coupling and climax while showing off the most fashionable kimono styles, hairdos, and accessories. These designs have become iconic symbols of erotic art and represent a strain of hedonistic beauty in Japanese culture often ascribed to folk tradition, Shinto naturalism, and the absence of Christian or Islamic concepts of sin and modesty.

Just as the common people enjoyed the world of *iro* without restraint during the Edo period, consumers of mass-market manga and anime today are comfortable with depictions of sexuality, in all its forms and variations, that would be inconceivable in their Western counterparts.

chic

粋

IKI

Iki is more an aesthetic of behavior than of appearance. To be iki *is to be smoothly styled, with nothing out of place or left to chance. It is a state of refinement entirely dependent on the person who embodies it.*

A person who is *iki* (often translated as "chic") understands the worlds of *iro* ("eroticism") and *tsuya* ("polish, refinement") *Iki* represents the slightly show-off "dandyism" of the Edo period and tends toward the stark and bold without being gaudy or excessive. It is a precursor of what is today called "Japanese cool."

But *iki* is also an attitude that can be described as a form of thoughtfulness of one person toward another. Let's imagine that, in the Edo period, a person takes part in a robbery in order to buy medicine for his sick mother. The judge, rather than sending the guilty person to prison, arranges a job for him.

This sympathetic move by the judge will be applauded by the common people as an act of *iki*.

An *iki* action is usually small in scale, but it has fine sensibility and a strong impact. In the example here, the judge is not trying to bring about a major change in the law; he is simply trying to help one unfortunate person. And that is exactly why this is a case of *iki*.

Similarly, let's say that we place a single camellia in a small vase. Even though this is a modest display of but a single flower, it gives people coming into the room a sense of peace, while also signaling the season of the year. This is an example of an *iki* arrangement.

Iki does not demand volume or eloquence. You can be *iki* by performing a small action to bring attention to something that would usually not be noticed.

profound tranquility

YŪGEN

In olden times, we paid attention to the darkness and listened to the bamboo swaying in the gentle breezes. Where is such a sense of profound tranquility, of yūgen, *today?*

As noted earlier, when closely observing the old and decaying (*sabi*) or that which is rustic and simple (*wabi*), a sensitive person can be moved beyond time to sense a surprising profundity in the universe. This sensation is called *yūgen*.

Yūgen may also be found in the uneasiness felt at the end of the day as darkness approaches, or in the subtle changes of the natural world as one looks into the tranquility and the abyss of space.

A profound tranquility is also part of the spirit world of the bewitched (*yō*). Here we see a glimmer of how *wabi* and *sabi* are connected to the aesthetic of death, as both these sensibilities reflect the eternal passage of time and with it decay and decline and the physical body's eventual transition to a world beyond this one.

Noh drama, which has played an important role in Japanese "high culture" since the Middle Ages, deliberately fosters and evokes this particular sense of beauty with scenes where the spirits of the dead speak of their trials.

connoisseurship

FŪRYŪ

The connoisseur, or fūryūjin, can sense the wabi and sabi of a place or object and leads a lifestyle that encourages the creation and appreciation of poems, artworks, and aesthetic conversation.

A tradition in Japan is called *tsukimi*, or moonviewing. In autumn, for example, friends gather on a veranda or some other outdoor space, and while observing the beautiful Harvest Moon in the nighttime sky, they write or recite poems. Or this what used to be done among the refined literati.

Being of a disposition to pursue such an activity and having the depth of learning and knowledge of poetry and tradition to profoundly understand and enjoy it is called *fūryū*, or "connoisseurhip."

Fūryū demands familiarity with one's culture, with its great books and poets and artists and craftsmen, but it is more than just that. The true *fūryūjin* ("person of *fūryū*") uses his discerning eye as a filter to observe things with the Japanese sense of beauty. He has all the core values and virtues described in the book at his disposal, and he uses them to evaluate both quality and intent.

The Japanese connoisseur is the epitome of refinement, but he understands deeply and is no dilettante.

The Chinese characters for *fūryū* mean "flow with the wind," and as the word suggests the *fūryūjin* is able to express his appreciation of traditional Japanese beauty in an elegant, seemingly effortless way.

index

索引

SAKUIN

Japanese Entries

和